SPORTS ACADEMY

Netball

Clive Gifford

FRANKLIN WATTS

LONDON • SYDNEY

First published in Great Britain in 2022 by The Watts Publishing Group

Copyright © The Watts Publishing Group 2022

Design and illustration: Collaborate Ltd

HB ISBN 978 1 4451 7845 5

PB ISBN 978 1 4451 7846 2

Printed in China

Note: At the time of going to press, the statistics and player profiles in this book were up to date. However, due to some players' active participation in the sport, it is possible that some of these may now be out of date.

Previously published by Franklin Watts as *Know Your Sport: Netball*

Franklin Watts

An imprint of Hachette Children's Group Part of The Watts Publishing Group Carmelite House

50 Victoria Embankment

London EC4Y 0DZ

An Hachette UK Company

www.hachettechildrens.co.uk

MIX
Paper from
responsible sources
FSC
www.fsc.org
FSC® C104740

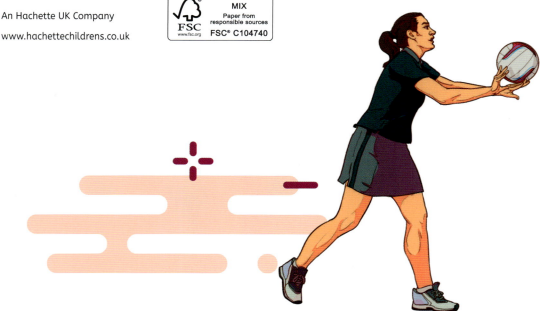

Please return or renew this item by the last date shown. There may be a charge if you fail to do so. Items can be returned to any Westminster library.

Telephone: Enquiries 020 7641 1300
Renewals (24 hour service) 020 7641 1400
Online renewal service available.
Web site: www.westminster.gov.uk

WITHDRAWN

City of Westminster

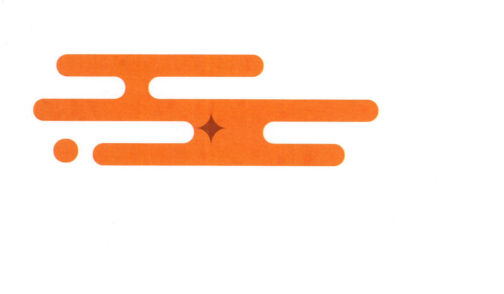

CONTENTS

WHAT IS NETBALL?

Netball is an exciting ball sport played by two teams each featuring seven players. The sport is incredibly fast-moving and calls on players to work hard as a team, make instant decisions and move sharply around the court.

The Aim of the Game

A full netball game lasts 60 minutes divided into four quarters of 15 minutes. There is a three-minute break between the first and second quarters and the third and fourth quarters. Half-time between the second and third quarters is five minutes long. Teams swap ends after each quarter. Teams pass and catch the ball but are not allowed to run or dribble with the ball. The court is divided into thirds (see page 13). When a team plays the ball from one end of the court to the other, the ball must be passed and caught at least once in each third.

The aim of the game is to score more goals than the other side. Tied games are allowed in most league competitions. In some knockout competitions, periods of extra time are played to decide which team wins. A goal is scored when the ball passes through the opposing goal hoop from above. The game is restarted each time with a centre pass taken from the centre circle.

Netball relies on players passing and catching the ball and moving into space to receive passes. These skills are relatively easy to understand but more challenging to show in a competitive game.

Umpires and Rules

Two umpires control the game, each being responsible for half of the court. The umpires rule on any faults that occur and can award a free pass, a penalty pass or a penalty shot (see page 38).

Netball is a non-contact sport and players cannot push or obstruct an opponent or wrestle the ball free. When an opponent has the ball, a defender cannot stand closer than 0.9 m from their opponent. A penalty pass or penalty shot may be awarded if contact or obstruction occurs.

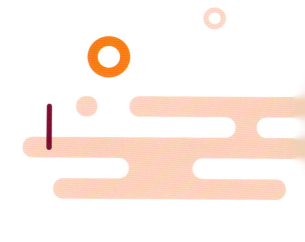

✗ Other Versions of Netball

Many countries have scaled-down versions of netball suitable for younger players. In England, High 5 Netball is popular in primary schools. It features five players a side playing on a smaller court using a smaller, size 4 netball. Players take part in four six-minute-long periods, known as quarters, and have four seconds rather than three to pass the ball. In Wales, a similar junior game called Dragon Netball is played whilst Scotland has Mini-Netball.

The History of Netball

Netball developed out of basketball, which was invented in 1891. By 1897 it was called netball, and in 1926 the All England Netball Association was formed. The game spread slowly from Britain to other countries and is now a booming team sport. Although best known as a game for girls and women, versions exist for men, mixed teams and for players in wheelchairs. In 1963, the first world tournament was held in England and featured 11 teams. The Netball World Championship is staged every four years in different countries around the world.

A player takes a shot. If successful, the game is restarted by a player from the other side of the centre circle.

TRAINING TO PLAY

Netball is a very athletic sport demanding great speed across the court, stamina to keep playing hard throughout the game and agility to jump high or stretch low. To play at your best, you need to train hard, prepare well and pay attention to your clothing and other kit.

Dress for Success

Whilst top teams may play in tight-fitting vests or all-in-one bodysuits, you should aim to wear clothing that is comfortable and loose-fitting to allow you to move freely. A short-sleeved polo shirt and a skirt, shorts or tracksuit bottoms are ideal. Players wear thick cotton sports socks which offer extra support and cushioning as they move around the court. As many junior netball games are played outside, a tracksuit is essential to keep your body warm before and after a match. Each player wears a bib with big letters on the front and back which represent their position, such as GS for Goal Shooter or C for Centre. Wearing jewellery is not allowed as a clash with another player may lead to injuries.

✗ Footwear

Netball is a high energy and high impact sport. The feet and lower legs take a pounding from running and jumping around on hard courts. So it makes sense to invest in trainers that are really comfortable, have plenty of cushioning inside for your foot and support your ankle and inside arch of your foot. The sole should have a grip suitable for the courts you play on. Always tie your shoes up tight and tuck the laces away neatly.

These (from left to right) groin, shoulder, back and finger stretches are just a small selection of stretches you should do before a game. Stretching helps prevent injury.

Preparation

Before training or playing a match, it is important to warm up and then stretch the major muscle groups in your back, shoulders and legs. Warming up can include exercises such as star jumps, jogging around the edge of the court and performing a few short, sharp sprints. Warming up helps to get blood pumping to your muscles and prepares you for the effort you will need to make in the game ahead. Follow your warm-up with stretching. Stretches should always be gentle and the stretch held for a few seconds before repeating. They will help you avoid injuries. Ask your coach to show you some stretches and supervise your stretching regime.

Netball Training

Netball training is in two parts which concentrate on skills and fitness. Skills training involves different drills suggested by a coach to help you improve your passing, catching, shooting, attacking and defending. Fitness training will depend on your age and ability level but often includes exercises designed to improve your sprinting speed over short distances.

PLAYERS AND POSITIONS

Netball is played on a court (see page 13) that measures 30.5 m long and 15.25 m wide. Compared to basketball the court markings are simpler, but important rules apply to which players can play in what parts of the court.

The Court and Goal

The court is divided into three equal-length thirds by two lines called transverse lines. The game starts from a 0.9-m diameter centre circle and restarts there after a goal is scored. The goal circle is a semi-circle with a radius of 4.9 m from the goalpost. The goalpost is 3.05-m high, fitted with a 380-mm-wide hoop with a trailing net. The sidelines and back line are included in the court area. For the ball to be 'out', it has to bounce on the floor or touch a wall or object outside of the court. If the ball goes out of court, the umpire awards a throw-in to the team who did not touch it last. A throw-in is taken from the point at which the ball went out of play.

Player Zones

Each team member has a specific position as shown on their bibs. Goal Attack (GA) and Goal Shooter (GS) are the only players allowed to shoot inside the goal circle. No player can travel throughout the entire court. Each playing position has a playing area in which they can operate. These are numbered on the diagram on page 13 and relate to the defending team's goal circle (1), their defending third (2), the centre third (3), their attacking third (4) and the goal circle they are attacking (5). If you step outside your permitted area the umpire will award a free pass to the opposition for offside.

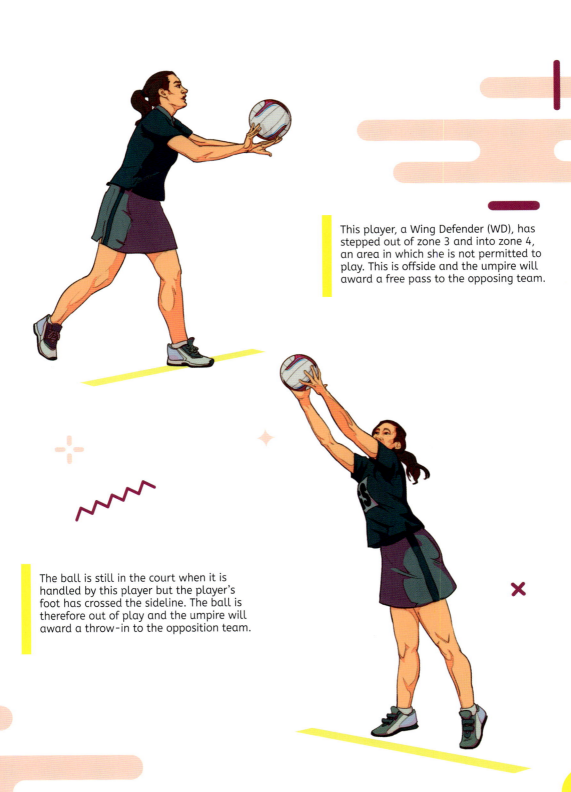

This player, a Wing Defender (WD), has stepped out of zone 3 and into zone 4, an area in which she is not permitted to play. This is offside and the umpire will award a free pass to the opposing team.

The ball is still in the court when it is handled by this player but the player's foot has crossed the sideline. The ball is therefore out of play and the umpire will award a throw-in to the opposition team.

Positions and Play

Each position brings its own responsibilities. The Goal Shooter (GS) and Goal Keeper (GK), for example, are mainly concerned with scoring or stopping goals. They play inside one goal circle and one third of the court. In contrast, the two Centres (C), one per side, play throughout the entire court except the goal circles and must be able to keep running throughout a game. A Centre tries to link with players such as the Wing Attack (WA) and Goal Attack (GA) to move the ball through the centre and attacking thirds to feed the ball into the goal circle.

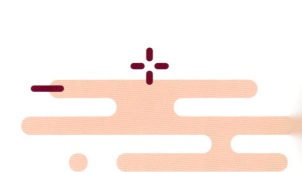

Who Goes Where?

Position	Bib Name	Area of Play
Goal Keeper	GK	1 and 2
Goal Defence	GD	1, 2 and 3
Wing Defence	WD	2 and 3
Centre	C	2, 3 and 4
Wing Attack	WA	3 and 4
Goal Attack	GA	3, 4 and 5
Goal Shooter	GS	4 and 5

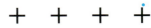

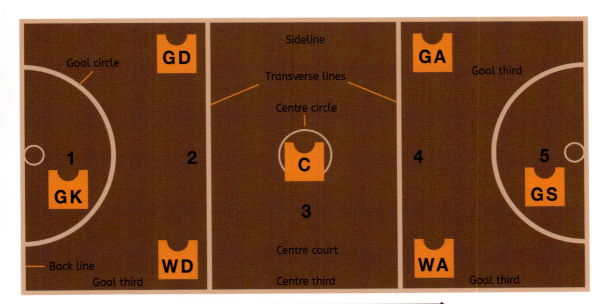

Goal circle

GD

Sideline

Transverse lines

Centre circle

GA

Goal third

1

2

C

4

5

GK

3

GS

Centre court

WA

Back line

WD

Goal third

Goal third

Centre third

Goal third

Direction of play

This diagram shows the five playing areas or zones on a court along with the typical starting positions for the different players in a single team.

CATCHING AND FOOTWORK

You and your team-mates will spend a lot of time practising the different types of pass. But without excellent catching skills, even the greatest pass is wasted. Catching needs a good eye and flexible hands. It also calls for good awareness of the footwork required to keep your balance while not breaking the rules.

Two-handed Catching

The most basic catch involves both hands taking the ball between chest and waist height. The catcher has to judge the speed and height at which the ball will travel to them and get into position to catch it comfortably. The catcher must not try to catch the ball with their hands and arms rigid as the ball is likely to bounce out of their grasp. When you practise catching, try to move towards the ball not away from it and watch the ball until it is safely in your hands.

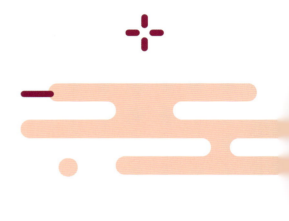

The Footwork Rule

This is a vital rule when catching the ball. When a player catches the ball, the first foot that touches the ground when they land is known as the grounded foot. While they are allowed to take that foot off the ground again, they must have passed and released the ball before that foot touches the floor again. Good netball players look to make their catches on the move, catching, landing and passing quickly all in one smooth set of movements.

✗ Two-handed Catching

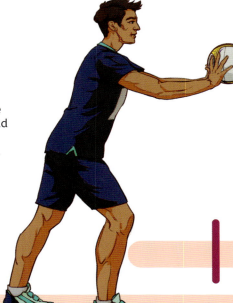

01 The catcher is balanced and upright with his eyes watching the arriving ball. He stretches out his arms to meet the ball with his fingers curved and spread widely apart. His arms are relaxed with the slightest bend in the elbows.

02 As the ball is caught, the catcher grips the ball around the back and sides. He cushions the ball's impact by drawing his hands and arms back towards his body. This helps secure the ball and gets the player into position to make a pass quickly.

One-handed Catching

Sometimes, the ball travels too high or too wide for you to make a two-handed catch. Rather than miss the ball, try to make a one-handed catch. The rules allow you to tap or bat the ball once in the air before trying to catch it. This can be useful to help bring the ball down. Aim to get your other hand up and onto the ball as soon as possible to make the ball secure. If the ball looks like it is going out of court, see if you can lean over the line with your feet behind it and claw the ball back with one hand. As long as your feet do not cross the line, you are still in court.

✗ **One-handed Catching**

01 This player cannot reach the ball with both hands. She jumps as high as she can and stretches up with her leading arm to bat the ball down once only so that she can get the ball under control.

02 As quickly as possible, she aims to get the ball in both hands safe and secure. This player has the ball positioned at shoulder height, ready to make a pass.

Catching Practice

Catching should be practised as often as possible. Once you have learned how to make passes, you and a friend can practise passing and catching together. Vary the passes so that the catcher has to react to the ball coming in at different speeds, heights and angles. As your catching and passing improve, start to move in between throws so that the pair of you work the ball up and down the court.

17

PIVOTING AND PASSING

Once you have control of the ball, you only have three seconds to release it. Spotting a passing opportunity and making the pass quickly and accurately are vital. Chest and overhead passes are frequently made throughout a game and are also used to restart the game from, for example, a throw-in.

Pivoting

With the ball securely in your hands you now have to deliver a pass quickly. Your eyes should be scanning the court looking for team-mates to pass to. Pivoting allows you to open up space on court by changing the direction of the game. Choose the direction you want to face and turn round, swinging your free leg whilst swivelling on the ball of one foot. This pivot foot has to stay in contact with the floor until after you have released the ball. The other foot, though, can move or step any number of times within the three seconds you have to make a pass. Your upper body should be kept as still as possible during a pivot.

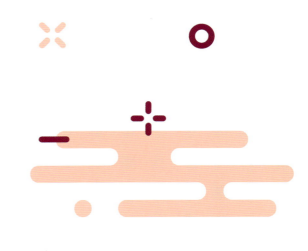

✗ Pivot and Pass

01 This player has control of the ball. With her head up, assessing the game, she decides to pivot round to her left. Swivelling on the ball of her right foot, she steps round with her left foot.

02 As she spots an opportunity for a chest pass (see page 21), the player plants her right foot and gets balanced. At the same time she has brought the ball up to her chest with her elbows bent ready to push forwards.

03 The player pushes both arms out sharply, with her elbows close to her side. Keeping her eyes on their target, she releases the ball with a flick of her wrists. Her hands follow through, pointing where the ball has travelled.

✗ The Overhead Pass

01 The pass starts with the ball held above the player's head with her elbows bent. Her hands are around the sides of the ball with the thumbs to the back.

02 The player throws the ball forwards by straightening her elbows and swinging them forward from the shoulder. She releases the ball with a flick of her wrists and fingers so that they are pointing to her target.

The Chest Pass

This two-handed pass is made from chest height. It is one of the quickest passes to play and is commonly used over shorter distances. The ball is held by the fingers rather than the palms, with the thumbs behind the ball and the wrists bent backwards. Your elbows should be bent and almost level or just below the centre of the ball. Your arms push out forwards and, with a flick of the fingers, the ball should zip through the air flat or almost flat towards your receiver.

The Overhead Pass

The overhead pass can be useful for a high aerial ball over the head and arms of an opponent. It can also be used for a quick, flat pass when you have caught the ball high or over your head as your arms are already almost in position to make the pass. Sometimes, players attempt a jumping version of this pass to start the ball travelling from an even greater height.

Passing on the Move

Practise your pivoting and passing by standing in the middle of a 10 m or so chalked circle with two friends moving around the edge of the circle. Receive a pass from one player and pivot quickly to find and pass to the other player. Practise this 15 times, using chest passes and overhead passes, before swapping places with one of the other players.

OTHER PASSES

The shoulder, bounce and underarm passes should be practised as often as the chest and overhead passes. Whatever type of pass you use, remember not to bypass a complete third of the court or the umpire will award a free pass to the other team.

The Shoulder Pass

The shoulder pass is the best way to move the ball over a longer distance, such as from the very edge of the court to the opposing sideline. It is a one-handed pass so you need to have a secure grip on the ball.

The Shoulder Pass

01 The player controls the ball with both hands as he brings it up to just above shoulder level. He takes the ball back with his throwing hand spread around the back of the ball and the foot on his non-throwing side forward. He leans back a little.

02 The player propels the ball forwards with a strong push from his shoulder. His arm points in the direction of his target. He releases the ball just as his arm fully straightens and flicks his wrists and fingers as the ball leaves.

The Bounce Pass

The rules of netball only allow one bounce in a pass between players, but that bounce can be used to get the ball around a close marking defender and into a team-mate's hands. The key difference is that the ball is aimed downwards to bounce at a point a little further than halfway between the thrower and the receiver. The bounce pass is used mainly over short distances, especially when the halfway point between passer and receiver is to the side of a defender's feet – the hardest place for the defender to reach in a hurry.

✗ Wall Ball

You can practise all your passes even without any other players. Get permission to use a wall with plenty of space, away from roads and traffic. Either chalk up circular targets on the wall or stick or tape cardboard circles to the wall at different heights. Stand a few paces back from the wall and work on all your different passes, aiming to hit a particular target every time. Vary the distance you stand away from the wall as well.

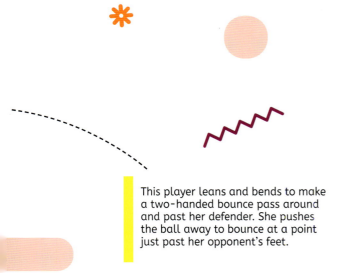

This player leans and bends to make a two-handed bounce pass around and past her defender. She pushes the ball away to bounce at a point just past her opponent's feet.

Low Passing

Most netball is played with the players staying tall, as they expect the ball to fly relatively high from chest, shoulder and overhead passes. This is why two low passes, the underarm and the bounce pass, can be very effective as they can surprise a defender.

The underarm pass is so named because the ball is bowled out underarm. It is best used over short distances and can sometimes push the ball underneath the arms of an outstretched defender. The pass is made with knees bent from a low position with an underarm swing of the ball. The hand supports the ball from underneath and releases the ball with a long, smooth follow-through of the arm.

MOVEMENT AND AWARENESS

Unlike basketball in which one player can dribble or throw the pass the length of the court, netball relies on a series of passes to move the ball. This calls for great teamwork as receivers must get themselves into good positions to receive passes.

Spotting Space

As a passer of the ball, pivoting helps you to see more of the court and assess options quickly. At the same time you rely on your team-mates to get free of their markers and move into space so that you can pass the ball to them. Receivers need to know in which direction the passer is facing and must be aware of any defenders marking them or in the way of a potential pass. As a receiver, your role is to spot useful space that is not blocked by opponents. If you spot a space, sprint hard into it but keep alert, watch the passer and be ready for the ball. If the pass does not come to you, start looking for the next opportunity to receive a pass.

This player is making a chest pass. She aims it ahead of her team-mate who is cutting sharply away from her marker to receive the ball.

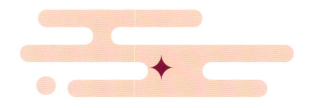

✗ Getting Free

With only three seconds on the ball, the passer is under pressure but so is the receiver. Defenders know this and aim to mark their player long enough to stop them receiving the pass. This is why getting completely free of your marker is vital. One of the simplest ways is to change your direction of movement. Head off fast in one direction, but then sharply cut back in another direction. This can wrong-foot a defender leaving you free long enough to catch the ball.

Fakes

Fakes are where you pretend to move in one direction, only to actually move in another. The key is to make your pretend move look convincing so that your marker believes you really are going that way. For example, to fake a move to your left, drop your left shoulder and bend your knees as if you're about to sprint that way. As your marker lunges or goes to follow you in that direction, push off hard from your left foot and head to the right.

The Reverse Pivot

Sometimes, a defender will mark you from the side. You may be able to sprint clear in the other direction, or you can try a reverse pivot. This is effectively a turn behind the back of the defender.

Dodging Your Marker

Your netball coach will suggest several different drills and games for you to practise getting free and into space to receive a pass. One simple game is to mark out an area 10 m by 10 m with cones in the corners. Play 2 v 1 with the one defender marking the receiver and the receiver trying to get free to receive a pass. The pair of players score a point for every three passes in a row they complete. The defender scores a point every time they intercept the ball or it leaves the square. After one side gets to eight points, swap the defender over with one of the attackers. You can build this game up with a bigger playing area and play 3 v 2 or 4 v 3 using similar rules.

✗ The Reverse Pivot

01 The Wing Attack (in the purple shirt) has her marker in front of her. She leans forward to convince the marker that she is heading to the left.

02 Pivoting on one foot, the player sharply turns behind the back of the defender. With the defender wrong-footed, she can receive the ball on the other side.

ATTACKING PLAY

Building an attack involves fast, accurate passing and well-timed movements from a team. The aim is to get the ball into the Goal Shooter's or Goal Attack's hands in the goal circle. Players use fakes, sprints and pivots to create the space required to receive the pass and keep an attack going.

Working Together

Communication and understanding between team-mates only comes through playing games and many hours of training and practice. Experienced team-mates use cues – signals between players to indicate where and when they are going to move. Two receivers can work together to create the space for a pass. For example, one receiver can sprint out of an area, taking their marker with them. This can create the space for a team-mate to run into to catch the ball.

✗ Pass and Move

Sometimes, the best time to get free is as a pass travels towards another team-mate. While the defenders are watching the ball, you have the chance to cut away sharply. Teams aim for fast, flowing movements in which a number of passes are made quickly in a row to get the ball into the goal circle. One simple example of such a move is the one-two or wall pass. This is where a player passes the ball to a receiver and sprints ahead of their marker to receive the ball back again.

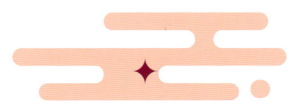

The attacking players in blue perform a one-two passing move to get the ball round and past a defender. The centre (far left) passes the ball then sprints forward to receive a pass.

Protecting Space

Sometimes, a passer may make the pass ahead of the receiver so that the receiver can cut away and collect the ball. Remember, only one bounce is allowed before the ball is collected. Another option is to protect space in front of you. Without fouling your marker, stand in front of them and use your body as a barrier. Your marker cannot reach that space without moving around you which takes time, enough time for you to move into that pocket of space to receive a pass.

✗ Protecting Space

01 The Wing Attack is standing to the side of her marker. By turning sharply she can use her body to protect the space to her side to receive a pass.

02 The Wing Attack makes her move. She turns and reaches out sharply to receive a pass. The marker is unable to get round the Wing Attack to prevent her receiving the ball.

Goal Circle

The Goal Attack and Goal Shooter are sometimes thought of as a team within a team. The two players need an excellent understanding with each other and with other players such as the Centre and Wing Attack that may be involved in the later stages of an attack. The Goal Shooter must be especially good at jumping and catching high balls and making very short, sharp sprints to receive a pass.

SHOOTING

The shooting technique in netball is relatively simple. But it takes a lot of concentration and excellent balance to shoot under pressure during a game. Players work really hard on practising their shooting technique so that it holds up under pressure or when they are tired.

The Static Shot

You have three seconds with the ball in your hands to take a shot. The static shot is the basic shot which is used most of the time. Aim for the ball to loop up in the air above the ring so that it can fall through it.

✗ The Static Shot

01 The player stands with his feet shoulder width apart and weight more on his back foot. He keeps his body straight and his eyes focused on the back of the ring. He balances the ball on the fingertips of one hand with the palm facing upwards and uses his other hand to steady the ball.

02 He lowers his arms a little so that the ball is above his head. Keeping his back straight and head up, he bends at the knees and then straightens his legs as if he was going to jump. This generates the force needed to send the ball into the air.

03 As his legs straighten, he lets go of the ball. He moves his arms as little as possible when he releases the ball but adds spin by flicking his wrists. He finishes the shot standing on tiptoe with his arms pointing towards the ring. He watches the ball's flight and is prepared to react if it rebounds off the goal ring.

Stepping and Shooting

Sometimes you may be forced to take the ball in a poor position to shoot, such as directly underneath the goal post. Remember that the footwork rule allows you to take a step providing you lift your landing foot up. You can take one step back and away from under the post with your landing foot off the ground. You can also choose to take a step to one side to get round the side of the Goal Keeper or Goal Defence. Shooting on one foot requires good balance but the shooting technique is very similar to the static shot.

Shooting Drills

However good teammates are at passing or how dominant they are in attack, if their two players in the shooting zone have a bad day, they cannot convert their superiority into points. Shooters, therefore, practise incredibly hard from every part of the goal circle. At first, you should just practise getting the ball in from your favourite positions in the circle to build accuracy and confidence. Then, start practising from different distances and angles and also with stepping and on one leg. If other players are around, practise with a defender in front of you to simulate match situations.

MARKING AND DEFENCE

In netball, if your team loses possession of the ball, focus on regaining the ball before your opponents get a chance to shoot at goal. All players on the team should become defenders until the ball is regained or a goal is conceded.

Marking

Most defence in netball is based on individual defenders marking individual attackers. Marking a player without the ball is all about denying them the space and opportunity to receive a pass. This has to be done legally without holding, pushing or obstructing your opponent. You must stand close to your opponent but in a position so that you can see both your opponent and the likely flight of the ball. Many players opt for a front marking position. They stand with their body partly in front of their opponent but at an angle, so that they can still move their head to watch their opponent and the ball. They try to keep on the balls of their feet ready to move in any direction to keep close to their opponent. Marking from the side forces your opponent into one area of the court.

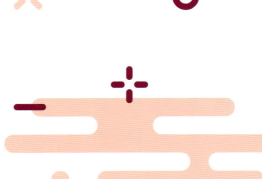

✗ Interception

01 The defender is approaching the attacker, keeping her knees bent with one arm up and one arm out to the side. She senses the passer raising the ball to make an overhead pass.

02 Reacting quickly, the defender jumps to block the pass. She will try to hold on to the ball, but if it falls loose, will aim to get to it first.

37

Defending Shots

A Goal Keeper and Goal Defence work as a team within a team to prevent the opposition having a good chance to shoot in the goal circle. But it is inevitable that such chances will occur at times during a game. If you are defending the player who is looking to shoot, your aim is to make as imposing and difficult a barrier as possible for the player to shoot over.

Stand tall with your arm up and palm out. Learn how to balance on one foot so that you can lean forwards to get your arm even closer. Another option is to time your jump to block or intercept a shot, but to do this you need to judge precisely when the shooter is going to release the ball. Whatever method you use, you have to stand 0.9 m away from the shooter, otherwise a penalty shot may be awarded by the umpire. If the shooter gets their shot away, immediately turn to face the post in case the ball misses and rebounds from the ring. Be prepared to jump to catch the rebound ball in the air.

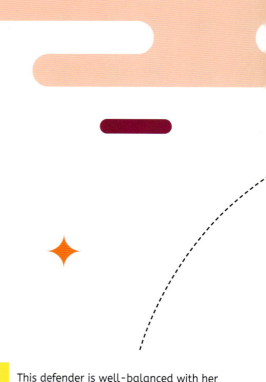

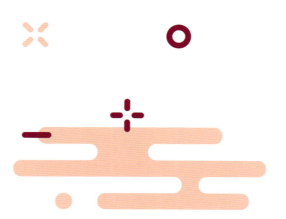

This defender is well-balanced with her body weight over her foot on the floor, her other leg and arm out to help her balance and her front arm leaning over the Goal Shooter.

Marking the Passer

When marking a player with the ball outside of the goal circle, be aware that your opponent may have a range of possible targets and can use different heights and angles of pass. Most markers opt to hold one arm up to stop the overhead or shoulder pass and the other arm out to the side to stop lower passes such as the bounce pass. Some players prefer to keep moving or jump up and down to distract the passer and reduce the space available to them.

TEAM DEFENCE

Whilst defence calls for excellent individual skills, it also requires players to work with each other as a team. Without good communication and teamwork, it will be hard to regain the ball or prevent the attacking side from scoring.

Working as a Team

Your one-on-one marking system (see page 36) is only as good as the weakest marker in the team. All players need to keep up the pressure on the opposing team. Keep communicating with your team-mates and be aware of sudden moves. Never complain about or abuse a team-mate who lets their opponent get free. It happens to all players. Good teamwork in defence may pressure the opposing side into throwing a weak or inaccurate pass. A defender who is aware of the game and reacts quickly may be able to intercept the ball in the air or on the ground and steal possession for her team.

Double Teaming

Normally, marking is one-on-one, but sometimes, a team may decide to put two markers on one opponent. This may occur in the goal circle if one of the shooting opponents is proving exceptionally accurate. Double teaming helps stop that opponent receiving the ball but will leave another opposing player free, so it is only used in some situations.

Spotting a slow, high pass, this defender has timed her run and jump to intercept the ball.

Zone Defence

Some teams use an alternative to one-on-one marking by marking an area of the court instead. This is known as zone defence. It may be used for a short period to disrupt play or to force a turnover in possession by making it hard for the attacking team to find a pass. Zone defence requires players who are skilled at holding their position, focusing on the movement of the ball and reacting to make a block or interception.

In this four-player zone, the Centre and Wing Defence patrol the front edge of the goal circle making sure they do not step into the circle. Together with the Goal Keeper and Goal Defence inside the circle, they aim to make a pass to the Goal Shooter impossible.

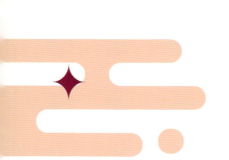

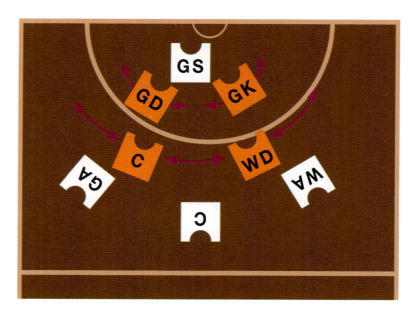

Full Court Zone

Sometimes, teams flood the centre third of the court with five players (Wing Defence, Goal Defence, Centre, Goal Attack and Wing Attack), the maximum number of players in that zone. This is called a full court zone. The Goal Shooter attempts to pressurise the opponent looking to pass the ball into the central third of the court whilst her five team-mates make it very hard for the opposing team to receive a pass and pass their way through.

STATISTICS AND RECORDS

World Netball Championship

Year	Winners	Runners-Up	Third Place
1963	Australia	New Zealand	England
1967	New Zealand	Australia	South Africa
1971	Australia	New Zealand	England
1975	Australia	England	New Zealand
1979	1st equal:		
	Australia	New Zealand	Trinidad and Tobago
1983	Australia	New Zealand	Trinidad and Tobago
1987	New Zealand	Trinidad & Tobago	Australia
1991	Australia	New Zealand	Jamaica
1995	Australia	New Zealand	South Africa
1999	Australia	New Zealand	England
2003	New Zealand	Australia	Jamaica
2007	Australia	New Zealand	Jamaica
2011	Australia	New Zealand	England
2015	Australia	New Zealand	England
2019	New Zealand	Australia	England

Commonwealth Games Netball

Year	Gold Medal	Silver Medal	Bronze Medal
1998	Australia	New Zealand	England
2002	Australia	New Zealand	Jamaica
2006	New Zealand	Australia	England
2010	New Zealand	Australia	England
2014	Australia	New Zealand	Jamaica
2018	England	Australia	Jamaica

2021 World Rankings

1. Australia
2. New Zealand
3. England
4. Jamaica
5. South Africa
6. Malawi
7. Uganda
8. Scotland
9. Wales
10. Trinidad and Tobago

Most World Championship Wins
Australia (11)

GLOSSARY

Attacking team
The team in possession of the ball.

Back line
The boundary lines at each end of a netball court.

Centre circle
The small circle in the centre of the court from where play is started or restarted after a goal is scored.

Centre court
The middle third of the court.

Cues
Signals made by one attacker to another to indicate where and when they want the ball passed.

Double teaming
When two players mark a single opposing player.

Fake
Also known as a dummy. A fake is when a player pretends to move or throw the ball in one direction but actually moves or throws in another direction. A fake is designed to trick an opponent.

Footwork rule
The rule which restricts the movement of the player in possession of the ball.

Free pass
A pass awarded to the opposing team for a penalty incurred.

Goal circle
The name of the circle around the goalpost which marks the scoring zone.

Marking
This is where one defender stands close to and shadows an opponent, attempting to prevent them receiving the ball or making a pass.

Obstruction
When an opposition player blocks any movement that interferes with a pass or shot. A penalty pass or shot is awarded to the obstructed team.

Offside
A call made by an umpire when a player leaves the parts of the court they are allowed to play in. A free pass is awarded to the opposition.

Pivoting
When a player swivels round on one foot to place the other foot in a new position.

Throw-in
Used to bring the ball back into court when it has gone out of play.

Transverse lines
The two lines dividing the court into thirds.

Zone defence
A method of defending where a team attempts to defend a specific area of the court to intercept the ball.

FURTHER INFORMATION

www.england-netball.co.uk

The official website for netball in England. The website contains news and profiles of England teams and details of summer camps, umpiring and contacts for netball clubs all over the country. It also contains links to all the Superleague clubs.

www.netball.com.au

The homepage of Netball Australia, this is a website packed with features on the national sides, the Commonwealth Bank Trophy for major clubs and, under the resources section, a complete list and scores of every game played by the national team.

www.netball.sport

This is the Internet home of the International Federation of Netball Associations (IFNA), the body that runs world netball.

www.netballnz.co.nz

The official website of the New Zealand netball team. Follow all the latest action and news from the Silver Ferns camp here along with news of competitions from internationals to New Zealand secondary schools.

www.netballscotland.com

The official home of Scottish netball with details of Scotland's national and junior sides and details of junior coaching and playing schemes.

www.walesnetball.co.uk

Homepage of the Welsh Netball Association, this website contains news of Welsh league netball as well as news of Dragon Netball for younger players and a fund of coaching tips presented in PDFs for you to download and enjoy.

Note to parents and teachers: every effort has been made by the Publishers to ensure that these websites are suitable for children, that they are of the highest educational value, and that they contain no inappropriate or offensive material. However, because of the nature of the Internet, it is impossible to guarantee that the contents of these sites will not be altered. We strongly advise that Internet access is supervised by a responsible adult.

INDEX

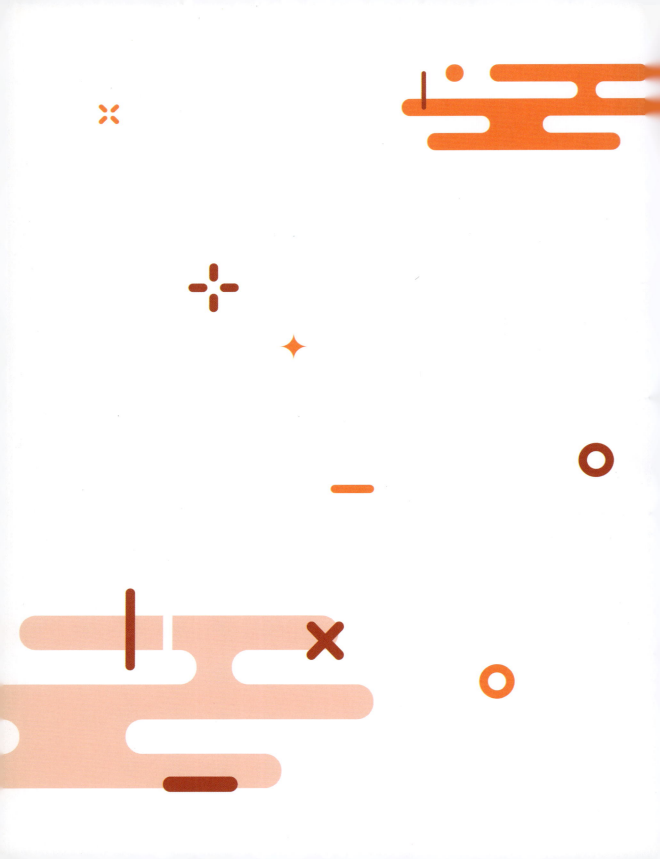